NOVICE TO SUCCESS:

MASTERING BUSINESS GROWTH WITH LITTLE OR NO EXPERIENCE, USING EXPERT STRATEGY.

JESSE N. DAVIS

COPYRIGHT PAGE

DEDICATION PAGE

To all aspiring entrepreneurs who are unafraid to pursue their ambitions,

This book is written in your honor.
May it serve as a source of inspiration for you as you traverse the world of business expansion.
To individuals with little or no experience, may the information on these pages instill confidence and empower you to take bold strides forward.

May this book be a source of wisdom, feeding your entrepreneurial spirit, for tenacious learners who desire information and advancement.
May it feed your fire as you leave your imprint on the world as risk-takers and trailblazers who dare to disrupt the norm.

This book is dedicated to my loved ones and mentors, whose continuous support keeps me going, and to the power of dreams.

This dedication is also dedicated to you, the dreamers and doers who turn possibility into reality, with heartfelt thanks and the highest respect.

THANK YOU FOR YOUR PURCHASE!

- [JESSE N. DAVIS]

TABLE OF CONTENT

INTRODUCTION

Aspiring business owners frequently find themselves at a disadvantage in a world where skill and experience are highly valued. The path of business can frequently resemble a complex and intimidating maze, with seasoned veterans appearing to have all the keys to success. What if, though, I were to suggest that your lack of experience might be your greatest strength? What if I were to provide a route that makes it possible for new business owners to succeed in a manner that is both straightforward and transformative?

On this fascinating voyage, we'll explore the undiscovered zone where daring, imagination, and a need for knowledge collide. Get ready to let go of the idea that success is only for the experienced. Here, we'll share our exclusive tips on embracing your inexperience as an entrepreneur and using it as fuel for rapid growth. Enter a world where mistakes are turned into lessons, where opportunities arise out of fear, and where uncharted territory becomes your playground. Learn how to rewrite the rules of the game, uncover overlooked opportunities, and think differently. Together, we'll break the mold of conventional success tales and create a story that is entirely original to you.

We're glad you're here, and welcome to the magical world of "Scaling from a Novice to Success; Mastering Your Business with Expert Strategies. With little or no experience." This fascinating adventure demonstrates the effectiveness of using your lack of expertise as a powerful weapon.

If you enjoy this book, kindly leave a review for it on Amazon to encourage the Author to write more of its kind.

THANK YOU FOR YOUR PURCHASE!

CHAPTER 1

THE POWER OF INEXPERIENCE

As an Entrepreneur Rookie, you have distinct qualities that can aid you in prospering when developing your firm. Even though entrepreneurs rookies can lack insight, they convey new viewpoints and innovative strategies to their organizations. Their courage permits them to tackle problems and do new things, which can prompt leaps forward.

They are consistently worried students, responding quickly to alterations on the lookout. Being adaptive and versatile assists them in changing their techniques based on the situation. Their passion and energy are infectious, pulling in supporters and financial backers. They approach new companies and are available to seek advice from seasoned tutors. By embracing these powers, inexperienced business visionaries can overcome hurdles and take remarkable steps toward development.

Added negatives to their being unpracticed. Business professionals who are fresh to the game could not have the same degree of industry information or organizations as those who have been in the business for longer. They may likewise discover it tougher to get subsidies or stand out from possible clients. Notwithstanding, with the appropriate perspective and approach, freshness can be transformed into a positive.

The following are several approaches to profiting from your incapacity as a business visionary:

EMBRACING THE BEGINNER'S MINDSET

Let me briefly share with you a story about a young and daring dreamer named Alex, who abandoned his usual 9-6 job and started on an entrepreneurial adventure armed with only one thing: the strength of a beginner's attitude.

Inexperienced yet undeterred, Alex turned his lack of understanding into an advantage.

Alex was unburdened by preconceived preconceptions, free to explore unexplored places, and challenge the status quo with curiosity as his compass, Instead of being held back by a fear of failure, Alex saw it as a chance to learn and grow.

With each setback, Alex learned crucial insights, transforming them into stepping stones towards future triumphs.

Guided by mentors and fueled by a hunger for wisdom, Alex's creative ideas shone brightly, establishing his business apart from the mass competition. Alex's narrative became a light of hope, encouraging those that followed suit, that beneath the unknown lurks the remarkable, ready to be discovered by those who dare to embrace the wonder of a beginner's mind.

Embracing a beginner's attitude provided Alex with the opportunity to ask daring questions, challenge assumptions, and pioneer new techniques.

In the end, Alex could view his inexperience as an opportunity rather than a hindrance that catapulted him to great success.

Nothing prohibits you from also turning your inexperience into a wonderful success story, just as Alex did. Your journey starts when you adopt a beginner's mindset.

● WHAT DO I MEAN BY ADOPTING YOUR BEGINNER'S MINDSET YOU WOULD ASK?

Embracing the beginner's mindset involves having an open and eager approach to learning, no matter how much experience you have. It's about being curious, asking questions, and being willing to try new things. Instead of assuming you already know everything, you approach circumstances with a fresh perspective and a desire to develop. When you adopt the beginner's mindset, you recognize that there's always something new to learn and that it's normal to make mistakes along the way. You're open to comments and seek guidance from those who can help you develop. You're not scared to venture outside your comfort zone and think differently.

It helps you unlock your creativity, adaptability, and potential. You're not restricted by what you already know or what others anticipate from you. It's a continual attitude of growth and learning that helps you discover new chances and accomplish greater success in life.

RECOGNIZING THE BENEFITS OF BEING A ROOKIE ENTREPRENEUR

Being a rookie entrepreneur comes with certain benefits that can help you succeed. In simple terms, they are:

1. *Fresh Perspective*: As a rookie, you bring fresh insight to the table. Without preconceived preconceptions, you can approach difficulties with new and imaginative answers that others might ignore.

2. *Willingness to Take Risks*: Without prior failures weighing you down, you're more open to taking measured risks. Embrace this fearlessness and grasp possibilities that can lead to growth and success.

3. *Quick Learning*: As a novice, you have a natural curiosity and willingness to learn. Embrace your passion for knowledge and adaptability, seeking out learning opportunities to stay ahead.

4. *Adaptability*: Rookies have the advantage of being flexible and adaptive. Without rigid frameworks, you can swiftly modify tactics to reflect changing market conditions and guarantee your organization remains relevant.

5. *Genuine Passion*: Your authentic excitement for your business is contagious. Embrace and express your enthusiasm, since it draws customers and sets you apart from competitors.

6. *Networking Opportunities*: Being new helps you connect with others in the entrepreneurial sector. Embrace networking, as it opens doors to lucrative relationships, insights, and growth opportunities.

7. *Mentorship*: Seek counsel from experienced mentors who can offer helpful insight. Embrace their mentorship to obtain insights, handle problems, and accelerate your learning.

Conclusively, identify and embrace the perks of being a rookie entrepreneur. Your new viewpoint, willingness to take risks, quick learning abilities, adaptability, real passion, networking opportunities, and mentorship can be great assets on your route to success. Embrace your rookie status and exploit these advantages to create your impact in the entrepreneurial environment.

OVERCOMING THE FEAR OF INEXPERIENCE

Fear of naiveté might be overpowering for aspirant business visionaries, but it should not prevent you from pursuing your goals. Here are a few methods to help you overcome your fear and thrive as a new company visionary:

Adopt a Learning Mentality: Rather than viewing newness as a flaw, consider it an opportunity to learn and grow. Accept the perspective of a beginner, where curiosity and openness drive your actions. Approach problems from a fresh perspective, seeking clarification on critical concerns and seeking guidance.

Begin with Small Steps: Divide your ambitious goals into smaller, more manageable tasks. By taking small steps, you can gain valuable experience and build certainty along the way. Every small accomplishment will propel you forward and strengthen your belief in your abilities.

Look for Information and Assets: Concentrate on learning more about your industry, business necessities, and appropriate skills. Use books, online courses, studios, and system administration events to expand your knowledge. Surround yourself with tutors, professionals, and a strong local community who can provide guidance and support.

Accept Mistakes and Disappointment: Recognize that mistakes are a normal part of the learning process. Accept them as opportunities for growth and learning. Dissect what went wrong, extract lessons from the experience, and use those lessons to improve your future projects.

Identify and Use Your Unique Talents:

As a new entrepreneur, identify and utilize your unique talents. Whether it's your fresh ideas, excitement, or unique point of view, these attributes can set you apart from the crowd. Concentrate on honing and applying these qualities to achieve a positive outcome in your business.

Create a Stable Organization: Surround yourself with colleagues who share your pioneering spirit. Join networks, attend system administration events, and look for tutors who may provide important bits of knowledge and support. Collaboration with others can help you overcome challenges and stimulate growth.

Value Flexibility and Consistent Learning: Value the fact that innovative adventure is a never-ending educational experience. Maintain adaptability and be open to developing your methods in response to market criticism and changing conditions. Accept a growth mindset that welcomes new opportunities and challenges.

By adopting a learning mindset, making small steps, seeking information, embracing mistakes, leveraging attributes, establishing an organization, and embracing flexibility, you may overcome your fear of inability and embark on an effective pioneering venture. Remember that every outstanding businessperson began as a novice, and with sincerity and consistency, you may achieve your goals.

GET THE MOST OUT OF YOUR BEGINNER'S MINDSET

On your entrepreneurial path, your beginner's mindset a great asset. Let's walk through the process of making the most of it with these six major attitudes in your beginner's mindset:

Embracing Curiosity and Having a Fresh Perspective: Approaching each situation with curiosity and a desire to learn, asking questions, exploring new ideas, and seeking out different perspectives allows you to discover innovative solutions and opportunities that others may overlook. Push yourself to think beyond the box and bring new ideas to the table. Your distinct point of view can inspire innovative solutions and help you stand out in a crowded industry.

Learn from your Mistakes: Accept that mistakes and failures are a natural part of the learning process. Setbacks should be viewed as great learning opportunities rather than as a source of discouragement. Analyze what went wrong, draw lessons from the experience, and apply what you've learned to develop and grow.

Establish a Solid Network: Surround yourself with mentors, peers, and experts who can provide you with useful advice and assistance. Meet other entrepreneurs, go to industry events, and look for mentorship possibilities. Learn from those who have gone before you and use their experience to enhance your progress.

Taking Calculated Risks: Your beginner's mindset permits you to take calculated risks without fear of failing in the past. Accept measured chances and be willing to venture outside of your comfort zone. This willingness to take chances might result in breakthrough moments and new opportunities.

Maintain Humility and Open-Mindedness: Keep in mind that there is always more to learn and explore. Maintain your humility and open-mindedness as you gain experience. Accept feedback and be willing to change your strategies in response to fresh knowledge. This willingness to learn regularly will keep you nimble and adaptable in a fast-changing corporate scene.

Remain Passionate and Persistent: Passion and excitement fuel your beginner's mindset. Maintain your enthusiasm for your business and allow it to propel you ahead, even when faced with obstacles. Maintain your perseverance and resilience, understanding that every setback is an opportunity to learn and improve.

You may harness the power of curiosity, new ideas, and a readiness to learn by making the most of your beginner's attitude. Accept failure, create a strong network, take smart chances, remain humble, and be enthusiastic and persistent. You can use these tactics to maximize the potential of your beginner's mindset and pave the route for business success.

CHAPTER 2

LAYING THE FOUNDATION

For inexperienced business owners, laying the groundwork is essential. Before beginning the venture, it entails taking the time to plan and prepare. Entrepreneurs can set themselves up for long-term success by laying a strong foundation. Setting clear corporate goals and vision is a crucial component of building the foundation. This aids business owners in determining their mission and target demographics. Understanding the issue they hope to address enables entrepreneurs to focus their efforts in one particular direction, making it simpler to make decisions as their organization expands.

The creation of an effective company plan is another crucial component. This plan serves as a road map by detailing the goals, tactics, and projected financials of the company. Conducting market research, analyzing the competition, and determining financial viability is necessary for developing a thorough plan. It aids business owners in understanding probable difficulties and creating backup strategies.

It is essential to comprehend the market and the target audience. Entrepreneurs can uncover and comprehend their potential clients' wants and preferences through market research. This data is necessary for properly adapting goods or services to match customer requests. Entrepreneurs improve their chances of success by correctly positioning their companies and setting themselves apart from rivals.

Obtaining funding and resources is another aspect of laying the foundation. An entrepreneur's position while looking for finance or luring potential partners or staff is strengthened by a solid foundation. Before committing capital, lenders and investors frequently want a thorough business plan and proof of market research. Having a solid foundation increases the possibility of gaining financial support by establishing trustworthiness.

Laying a solid foundation also makes it easier to mitigate risks and make educated judgments. Entrepreneurs can effectively manage risks by developing ways to identify them early on. As the firm develops, the foundation offers a knowledge base for making wise decisions. Entrepreneurs can review their planning and research to evaluate fresh opportunities, deal with obstacles, and modify their strategy as necessary.

And finally, it's crucial to develop a professional network. Entrepreneurs can get helpful advice, insights, and prospective partnerships via networking with colleagues in the sector, mentors, advisers, and clients. Access to resources, knowledge, and opportunities through these connections may help to hasten the expansion of a business.

The likelihood of long-term success is increased for novice business owners who build a solid basis for their enterprise. They are given a clear road map, which lowers uncertainty and enables them to make well-informed decisions, ultimately promoting growth and sustainability. Let's go over the crucial elements that can assist a novice build a strong foundation for their business:

SETTING CLEAR GOALS AND OBJECTIVES

Setting defined goals and objectives is vital for increasing success in business, especially for rookie entrepreneurs. Here's a basic step-by-step strategy to help you develop clear goals and objectives:

Start by defining your broad vision for the business: What do you want to achieve in the long run? This will guide your goal-setting approach. Next, identify particular areas that need to increase for your firm to prosper, such as boosting sales, enhancing efficiency, or extending your customer base.

When setting goals, use the SMART goals formula:

This means **SMART, MEASUREABLE, ACHIEVABLE, RELEVANT, AND TIME - BOUND**.

Be clear about what you want to accomplish, create quantifiable targets, make sure they're reasonable and relevant to your business, and set a timetable for accomplishing them. Break down your goals into smaller, actionable targets. These are the measures you need to follow to attain your goals. Assign duties and set timeframes for each goal. Regularly assess your goals and objectives to track progress and make adjustments when required.

It's usually useful to seek advice and mentorship from experienced entrepreneurs who can provide significant insights. Track your progress using metrics or key performance indicators, and celebrate your victories along the way. Remember to stay focused, adaptive, and devoted to ongoing growth.

By following these simple steps, defining clear goals and objectives that connect with your vision and paving the road for increasing success in your business would be a piece of cake.

FINDING YOUR UNIQUE VALUE PROPOSITION

A strong value proposition should be clear, succinct, and customer-focused. It should express why your business is the best choice and why clients should choose you over the competition. Finding your distinct value offer is an ongoing effort. Continuously refine and communicate it across your marketing platforms, website, and consumer interactions. Your value proposition should be original, distinctive, and focused on giving value to your customers.

By analyzing your target audience, exploiting your capabilities, and being alert to the market, you can design a compelling value offer that sets your firm apart and draws clients.

To discover your unique value proposition, follow these steps:

Understand your target audience by learning about their wants and preferences. Start by acquiring a comprehensive understanding of your target audience. Who are they? What are their wants, desires, and pain points? Understanding your audience will help you personalize your value package to their demands.

Analyze your competition to uncover possibilities to stand out. Research your competition and identify what they provide. This will help you uncover gaps in the industry and find possibilities to stand out. Look for places where you may provide something new or better than your competition.

Identify your strengths and distinctive qualities. Take a thorough look at your business and find the distinctive skills, qualities, or resources that set you apart. These could include knowledge, innovative ideas, outstanding customer service, a specialized niche emphasis, or a new method of solving an issue.

Determine the particular value you bring to clients and how you handle their problems better than anybody else. How does your product or service solve their problems or meet their demands better than everyone else? Focus on the benefits and outcomes that customers can expect by choosing your business.

Craft a clear and appealing statement that communicates your distinctiveness. Once you've found your distinct value proposition, distil it into a clear and appealing statement. Convey what makes you different and why they should choose you. Use straightforward and accessible language to guarantee your message resonates with your target audience.

Test your value proposition with clients and adjust it depending on their input. You can discuss your value proposition with a limited group of clients or trusted individuals and receive feedback. Pay attention to their emotions and suggestions. Use this input to tweak and strengthen your value proposition until it successfully expresses your distinct worth.

Conduct detailed market research and seek regular client feedback. Perform a SWOT analysis to understand your business's **Strengths, Weaknesses, Opportunities, and Threats**. Evaluate your business's strengths, weaknesses, opportunities, and threats (**SWOT analysis**). This exam will help you identify areas where you shine and where you may need to improve. Leverage your strengths and solve deficiencies to generate a convincing value proposition.

Focus on highlighting the benefits and outcomes clients may expect, and regularly analyze the market to stay current and change your value proposition as needed.

UNDERSTANDING YOUR TARGET MARKET AND AUDIENCE

Understanding your target market and audience is vital for the success of your business. It enables you to personalize your products, services, and marketing methods to fit their specific wants and preferences. Here's a simplified technique to help you understand your target market and audience:

1. *Define your target market*: Start by determining the exact group of people who are most likely to be interested in your products or services. Consider demographic data such as age, gender, locality, income level, and occupation. This helps you narrow down your

focus and establish customized marketing strategies.

2. *Conduct market research*: Gather facts and insights about your target market through market research. This can involve surveys, interviews, or evaluating existing data. Find out their preferences, purchase behavior obstacles, and motives. This information will guide your decision-making and help you adjust your offerings accordingly.

3. *Segment your audience*: Divide your target market into smaller segments based on shared features or demands. This allows you to generate more tailored marketing messages and tactics. For example, if you sell apparel, you may segment your audience by age group or style preferences.

4. *Develop buyer personas*: Create fictitious representations of your ideal clients, known as buyer personas. These personas comprise important features, preferences, and behaviors of

your target audience. By understanding their goals, challenges, and motivations, you may better address their requirements and design more effective marketing campaigns.

5. *Analyze competition*: Study your competitors to acquire insights into their target market and audience. Look at their marketing techniques, messaging, and customer interactions. This might help you uncover gaps or opportunities in the industry and differentiate your business.

6. *Listen and engage*: Actively listen to your target market and engage with them through social media, polls, or feedback channels. This helps you to obtain direct input, understand their problem spots, and establish partnerships. Use this information to continuously enhance your products, services, and customer experience.

7. *Monitor and adapt*: Stay updated about market trends, changes in customer behaviour, and developing demands. Continuously evaluate your target market and audience to guarantee your offers remain relevant. Be flexible to alter

your strategy and offers as necessary to suit evolving client expectations.

Understanding your target market and audience is an ongoing effort. Regularly evaluate and refresh your expertise to stay connected with their requirements and preferences. By acquiring a comprehensive understanding of your target market, you can successfully customize your business strategies and offers to suit their expectations, eventually driving success and customer happiness.

CREATING A SOLID BUSINESS PLAN

A business plan is an essential tool for the success and growth of your business. By following these steps, you can develop a comprehensive and effective business plan:
Start with an Executive Summary that provides a concise overview of your business. Summarize your mission, vision, and key objectives. This section gives readers a snapshot of what your

business is all about and helps set the tone for the rest of the plan.

Next, dive into the Company Description. Provide a detailed explanation of your business, including its legal structure, industry, and target market. Highlight what sets your business apart from competitors. Explain your unique selling points and why customers would choose your products or services.

Perform a thorough Market Analysis to gain insights into your industry, target market, and competition. Conduct market research to identify your target customers and understand their needs, preferences, and buying behaviour. Analyze your competitors to identify their strengths and weaknesses. This information will help you position your business strategically and identify growth opportunities.

Describe your Products or Services in detail. Explain what you offer and how it addresses the needs of your target market. Highlight the features, benefits, and any unique aspects that differentiate your offerings from competitors. If applicable, outline your product development plans or service delivery processes.

Outline your Marketing and Sales Strategy. Define your target audience and the marketing channels you will use to reach them. Explain your pricing strategy and promotional tactics. Detail your sales processes, distribution channels, and customer relationship management strategies. This section demonstrates how you plan to attract and retain customers.

Introduce your Organization and Management team. Describe the structure of your business and the roles and responsibilities of key members. Highlight their relevant experience and expertise, which contributes to the success of your business. If necessary, include an organizational chart to provide a visual representation.

Develop Financial Projections to estimate your business's financial performance. Include sales forecasts, cash flow projections, and profit and loss statements. Consider startup costs, operating expenses, and revenue projections. Conduct a break-even analysis and discuss any funding needs or financing options you may require.

Explain your Operations and Logistics. Provide details about your location, facilities, equipment, and suppliers. Describe your production processes and inventory management. If applicable, discuss any key partnerships or outsourcing arrangements that contribute to the smooth operation of your business.

Address the Risk Assessment and Mitigation strategies. Identify potential risks and challenges that could impact your business. Develop strategies to mitigate these risks, such as contingency plans, insurance coverage, or diversification strategies.

Additionally, address any legal or regulatory considerations that may affect your business operations.

Lay out an Implementation Plan that outlines the timeline and action steps needed to execute your strategies. Set specific goals, milestones, and deadlines. Assign responsibilities to team members and regularly track progress to ensure the effective implementation of your business plan.

Lastly, emphasize the importance of Evaluation and Review. Establish metrics and benchmarks to assess the performance of your business. Regularly review and update your business plan to reflect changing market conditions, new opportunities, and growth strategies. This ongoing evaluation ensures that your business plan remains relevant and aligned with your business goals.

Remember, a solid business plan serves as a roadmap for your business's success. It demonstrates your understanding of the market, defines your goals, and guides your actions. Keep your business plan updated and use it as a tool to make informed decisions, track progress, and communicate your vision to stakeholders.

CHAPTER 3

BUILDING A STRONG SUPPORT NETWORK

Building a strong support network is an essential ingredient for the success of any business. It is a strategic move that can propel your growth, provide valuable insights, and open doors to new opportunities. A robust support network consists of mentors, industry peers, skilled professionals, and potential investors who collectively contribute to your business's development.

Mentors offer guidance based on their experience, helping you navigate challenges and make informed decisions. Industry peers provide a sense of camaraderie, allowing for knowledge sharing and collaboration. Skilled professionals bring expertise in critical areas, ensuring your business is well-equipped to tackle complex tasks. And investors can provide the necessary financial backing to fuel your expansion plans.

Building a support network requires active participation, networking, and a genuine willingness to contribute to others' success. By cultivating meaningful relationships and reciprocating support, entrepreneurs can tap into a vast pool of resources, advice, and opportunities. In this interconnected business landscape, a strong support network acts as a catalyst, enabling businesses to scale and thrive in an ever-evolving market. Below are four ways you can build a strong support network for yourself and your business:

SEEKING GUIDANCE FROM THE RIGHT MENTORS

Seeking guidance from the right mentors is a key factor in personal and professional growth. Mentors offer valuable insights, knowledge, and perspective gained from their own experiences, which can help you navigate challenges and make informed decisions.

When searching for mentors, consider individuals who have expertise and success in your field or a related industry. Look for someone who aligns with your values and goals and has a genuine interest in supporting your growth. Seek mentors who are approachable, open to sharing their knowledge, and willing to provide honest feedback.

Establishing a mentoring relationship requires proactive effort. Communicate your objectives and expectations to your potential mentor, and express your gratitude for their guidance. Be prepared for mentorship sessions by coming up with specific questions or challenges you want to discuss. Actively listen to their advice, reflect on their insights, and implement the lessons learned in your own journey.

Remember that mentoring is a two-way street. Show your commitment and dedication by following up on their suggestions, keeping them updated on your progress, and seeking their input when needed. Additionally, consider offering your skills and expertise in return, as mentorship relationships can be mutually beneficial.

Seeking guidance from the right mentors can accelerate your learning curve, broaden your

perspective, and provide invaluable support on your entrepreneurial journey. Embrace the wisdom and guidance they offer, and leverage their insights to achieve your goals.
Here are a few listed importances and benefits of having the right mentors:

• *Knowledge and Experience*: Mentors possess a wealth of knowledge and practical experience in their respective fields. They have likely encountered similar challenges and can provide valuable insights on how to overcome them. Learning from their successes and failures can save you time, energy, and resources.

• *Expanded Network*: Mentors often have extensive networks and connections within your industry. By associating yourself with a respected mentor, you gain access to their network, which can open doors to new opportunities, partnerships, and introductions to influential individuals.

- ***Objective Feedback***: Mentors offer an objective perspective on your ideas, strategies, and decisions. They can provide constructive criticism and help you see blind spots or potential pitfalls that you may have overlooked. Their unbiased feedback allows you to refine your approach and make more informed choices.

- ***Personal Growth***: Mentors not only provide professional guidance but also support your personal growth. They can offer advice on work-life balance, personal development, and self-improvement. Their mentorship extends beyond business matters, helping you become a well-rounded individual.

- ***Inspiration and Motivation***: Having a mentor who has achieved success in your desired field can be highly inspiring and motivating. Their stories of overcoming challenges and reaching their goals can fuel your determination and belief in your own abilities.

- *Accountability and Support*: Mentors can hold you accountable for your actions and goals. They provide guidance, encouragement, and support to keep you focused and motivated. Knowing that someone with experience is invested in your success can push you to strive for excellence.

- *Continuous Learning*: Mentoring relationships provide ongoing learning opportunities. Through regular discussions, mentorship sessions, and exposure to their knowledge and experiences, you can continually expand your skills and expertise.

When seeking mentors, be proactive and approach individuals you admire and respect. Look for compatibility in terms of values, communication style, and availability. Remember that mentorship is a voluntary relationship, so be respectful of their time and commitments.

Building relationships with mentors requires effort and dedication. Show your appreciation, stay engaged, and demonstrate your willingness to learn and grow. By seeking guidance from the right mentors, you can accelerate your professional development, gain valuable insights, and increase your chances of success.

HOW TO MAKE AND LEVERAGE NETWORKING AND CONNECTIONS

Networking and connections play a crucial role in scaling your business to success. Here are some steps to help you make and leverage networking and connections effectively:

1. *Attend Industry Events*: Participate in conferences, trade shows, seminars, and networking events relevant to your industry. These gatherings provide opportunities to meet professionals, potential clients, partners, and investors. Be proactive in engaging with

attendees, exchanging contact information, and initiating conversations.

2. *Join Professional Associations*: Become a member of industry-specific associations or organizations. Attend their meetings, workshops, and social events. By actively participating, you can connect with like-minded individuals, stay updated on industry trends, and build relationships that can be beneficial for your business.

3. *Utilize Online Platforms*: Leverage online platforms, such as LinkedIn, Facebook,Twitter, or other social or industry forums, and social media groups, to expand your network. Engage in discussions, share valuable content, and connect with professionals in your field. Use these platforms to showcase your expertise and establish yourself as a thought leader.

4. *Seek Referrals*: Existing clients, partners, or colleagues can be valuable sources of referrals. Ask satisfied customers to refer your business to

their contacts. Foster strong relationships with partners and collaborators who can recommend your services to their network. Referrals can lead to warm introductions and help you gain trust and credibility in new circles.

5. *Nurture Relationships*: Building connections is not just about collecting business cards. Invest time and effort in cultivating meaningful relationships. Follow up with new contacts, send personalized messages, and stay in touch periodically. Offer assistance, provide value, and show genuine interest in their success. Building strong relationships creates a foundation for mutually beneficial collaborations.

6. *Provide Value*: Networking is not solely about what you can gain; it's also about what you can contribute. Offer your expertise, insights, or assistance to others in your network. Share valuable resources, make introductions, or provide support whenever possible. By being generous and helpful, you build a reputation as a

valuable connection and someone others will be more inclined to help in return.

7. ***Collaborate with Strategic Partners***: Identify businesses or individuals who complement your offerings and target the same audience. Collaborate on joint projects, cross-promotions, or co-creation of content. Partnering with strategic allies can expand your reach, leverage each other's networks, and create new growth opportunities.

8. ***Attend Entrepreneurial Events***: Engage with local startup communities, entrepreneurship centres, and pitch competitions. These events attract investors, mentors, and fellow entrepreneurs. Pitch your business, seek feedback, and connect with potential supporters who can help you scale your business.

9. ***Leverage Existing Connections***: Look within your current network for opportunities. Reach out to past colleagues, classmates, or acquaintances who may have connections or resources that can support your growth. Nurture

these existing relationships and leverage their knowledge and influence.

10. ***Be Authentic and Follow Up:*** Authenticity is key in networking. Be genuine, show interest in others, and listen actively. After meeting someone, make it a priority to follow up promptly. Send personalized follow-up messages, schedule meetings or calls, and explore ways to collaborate further.

Remember, networking is a continuous process. Regularly invest time and effort in expanding and nurturing your network. Be patient, as it takes time to build valuable connections. By leveraging networking and connections effectively, you can access new opportunities, gain support, and propel your business towards success.

COLLABORATING WITH LIKE-MINDED INDIVIDUALS

Collaborating with like-minded people can be a great way to grow your business. Here's how you can do it in simple steps:

1. *Find People Who Share Your Goals*: Look for individuals or businesses that have similar values and objectives to yours. They should want to achieve similar things as you do.

2. *Build Trust*: Get to know potential collaborators and see if you work well together. Make sure you trust and understand each other.

3. *Clarify Roles*: Decide what each person's responsibilities will be in the collaboration. Make sure everyone knows what they need to do.

4. *Communicate Openly*: Keep the lines of communication open and share updates

regularly. Talk about any issues that come up so you can solve them together.

5. *Use Each Other's Strengths*: Figure out what each person is good at and use those skills to your advantage. You can learn from each other and help each other succeed.

6. *Look for Mutual Benefits*: Make sure both sides benefit from the collaboration. It's important that everyone gains something and contributes to each other's success.

7. *Put Things in Writing*: Write down what you agree on so everyone knows what to expect. Include things like the work you'll do, how you'll handle money, and any other important details. It is always better to have legal backup contracts or agreements for your relationships.

8. *Check and Adjust*: Regularly see how things are going and make changes if needed. Talk to your collaborators about what's working and what can be improved.

9. ***Build Long-Term Relationships***: Collaborations can lead to long-lasting connections. Stay in touch with the people you work well with and support each other as your businesses grow.

By collaborating with like-minded people, you can achieve more together and make your business stronger. Just find the right partners, communicate openly, and focus on mutual success.

USING SOCIAL MEDIA AND ONLINE COMMUNITIES FOR YOUR BENEFIT

Utilizing online forums and social media may be likened to setting loose a digital blaze for your company. Here's how to use these alluring tools to spark your growth:

1. ***Find the Social Hotspots***: Identify the thriving social media sites and online

communities that attract your target market. Concentrate your efforts in the areas where your target audience is most likely to congregate and the digital buzz is the loudest.

2. *Start Regular Engagement*: Regularly fueling the flames of engrossing material can help you establish a burning presence on social media. Posts that inform, amuse, and encourage your readers to participate in the discussion will fuel the fire. Maintain a high heat and a blazing ember.

3. *Encourage Interaction*: Encourage interaction by actively engaging in dialogue with your followers. Authenticity and excitement are key when responding to remarks, messages, and mentions. You can create a sense of community that keeps your audience returning by stoking the conversation.

4. *Forge a Path with Valuable Content*: Set the online world on fire by disseminating worthwhile content that inspires interest and a want for more. Use educational blog pieces,

smokin' films, stunning infographics, and blazing how-to instructions to fan the flames. Let your material glow like a guiding light for knowledge.

5. ***Work together with social media influencers*** to create explosive cooperation with those who are leading the charge for influence in your sector. Join forces to promote your business to its sizable audience through guest appearances, interviews, or collaborative initiatives. Their support will ignite your company and draw a firestorm of new customers.
Join the burning depths of online forums, communities, and organizations that fuel the passions of your target audience.

6. ***Join the Burning Online Communities***: By contributing insightful information, starting conversations, and lending a helpful hand, add fuel to the fire. Make connections that will keep your company shining in the eyes of your neighbourhood.

7. *Ignite Curiosity with Hashtags*: Use current and pertinent hashtags in your social media posts to stimulate curiosity and fan the flames of exploration. Create a path to new audiences and allow your information to spread like wildfire, attracting interest from all parts of the online world.

8. *Light the Fire of Analytics*: Harness analytics' power to follow the trail of your social media success. To discover what piques the curiosity and motivates the involvement of your audience, examine the data flames. Use these insights to stoke the fires of your social media strategy and ignite the growth of your company.

9. *Create a Network of Wildfire Relationships*: Let social media networking sparks flare and create connections that shine. Engage peers, leaders in the industry, and possible partners. Make relationships that inspire collaborations and enlighten your road to success.

10. *Control the Flames of Reputation*: Keep an eye on the internet's reputational wildfire. Immediately and diplomatically respond to all comments, positive and negative. By promptly responding to complaints and demonstrating your dedication to client satisfaction, you may put an end to any criticism. Let your reputation shine like a trustworthy guiding light.

So let social media and online communities ignite a fire of possibility and growth for your company. Accept the heat, use the power, and watch as your success in the digital sphere ignites like a burning phoenix.

CHAPTER 4

LEARNING FROM FAILURE

Learning from failure is a vital component of personal and professional growth. While failure can be upsetting and disheartening, it gives essential lessons and opportunities for progress.

To effectively learn from failure, it is vital to have a development mentality. This involves viewing failure as a stepping stone to success rather than a dead end. It's vital to remember that failure is not a reflection of your worth or ability but an opportunity to learn and progress.

When faced with failure, take the time to assess the situation critically. Understand the elements that lead to the failure, such as your actions, decisions, external situations, or any other significant components. Identifying the core causes can help you prevent such blunders in the future.

Taking responsibility for your role in the failure is a vital stage in the learning process. Acknowledge your acts and decisions, assuming responsibility for the outcomes. By doing so, you can learn from your mistakes and take proactive efforts to prevent them from happening again.

One of the most crucial components of learning from failure is taking lessons from the experience. Reflect on what could have been done differently, which techniques were ineffective, and what abilities require work. These insights will aid you in making better decisions and taking suitable actions in the future.

Seeking feedback from trusted mentors, colleagues, or friends is also beneficial. They can offer new viewpoints, provide constructive criticism, and assist you develop a deeper understanding of the failure. Their input can be important in your growth and development.

Using the insights learned from failure, alter your approach and techniques. Refine your approaches, build new talents, or adjust your goals based on the lessons learnt. Failure can be a stimulus for innovation and improvement provided you are prepared to adapt.

Building resilience is key in rebounding back from setbacks. Cultivate a positive outlook, build coping skills, and practice self-care. Remember that setbacks are transient, and with determination, you can overcome them.
Apply the information gained from the failure to your future attempts. Use the insights and lessons learnt to make educated decisions, take reasonable risks, and continuously enhance your skills and abilities.

Embrace the principle of iteration and understand that success rarely arrives linearly. View failure as a natural part of the learning process and acknowledge that each failure puts you one step closer to success if you learn and iterate along the way.

Lastly, applaud the improvements you achieve, no matter how modest. Every step forward is a result of the lessons acquired from failure. By acknowledging your growth and achievements, you build confidence and drive to continue learning and aiming for success.

Note that, failure is not the end but an opportunity to learn, progress, and finally attain success. Embrace failure as a useful lesson on your journey towards personal and professional success.

EMBRACING A GROWTH MINDSET

Embracing a growth mindset is about knowing that your abilities and intelligence are not fixed attributes but can be improved through work and learning. It includes seeing problems as chances to learn and grow, and enduring in the face of setbacks. By embracing the process of learning and being positive, you can develop resilience and overcome hurdles.

Surrounding oneself with encouraging people and seeking ongoing learning will further increase your growth. Additionally, being open to change and adapting to new conditions will help you manage the ever-evolving environment of life and work. Embracing a development mindset helps you uncover your full potential and achieve personal and professional success.

ANALYZING AND LEARNING FROM MISTAKES

Analyzing and learning from mistakes is a transformative process of personal and professional development. It entails diving deep into the mistake, analyzing its causes, and extracting important insights. By accepting responsibility for your actions, you empower yourself to develop and adapt. The lessons acquired from mistakes act as guideposts for improvement, enabling you to polish your talents, boost decision-making, and optimize processes. Implementing these principles initiates a cycle of ongoing growth, moving you towards higher levels of achievement.

Seeking criticism from others creates collaboration and deepens your understanding of the mistake. By embracing this transforming process of analyzing and learning from failures, you create resilience, adaptability, and an unyielding dedication to improvement. The lessons learned help you identify opportunities for growth, whether they are related to abilities, decision-making, or processes.

Implementing these modifications based on the knowledge obtained sets you on a path of ongoing progress. Seeking feedback from others gives useful insights and varied viewpoints to increase your understanding. By embracing this constant process of analyzing and learning from failures, you build a mindset of growth and unlock your potential for greater achievement.

OVERCOMING SETBACKS AND CHALLENGES

Overcoming setbacks and adversities is a crucial ability that helps us thrive and achieve success. It involves a diverse set of methods to navigate through difficult conditions and emerge stronger. Here are some crucial elements to consider when it comes to overcoming setbacks and challenges:

1. *Adopt a Resilient mentality*: Cultivate a resilient mentality by viewing setbacks as temporary challenges and believing in your capacity to overcome them. This approach helps you stay motivated and focused on seeking solutions.

2. *Assess and Accept the circumstance*: Assess the setback or obstacle objectively, admitting the

truth of the circumstance without lingering on negativity or blaming. Acceptance allows you to transfer your efforts towards discovering positive answers.

3. *Seek Support*: Reach out to a network of supportive people, such as friends, family, or mentors, who may provide direction, advice, and encouragement. Their perspective and expertise can offer significant insights and assist you navigate through the problems.

4. *Break It Down and Prioritize:* Break the challenge into smaller, achievable tasks, then prioritize them based on importance and urgency. This strategy allows you to attack the issue step by step, making progress along the way.

5. *Stay Flexible and Adapt*: Remain adaptive and open to altering your goals or strategies when necessary. Being flexible allows you to explore other ways and develop inventive solutions to overcome barriers.

6. *Learn from Setbacks*: Embrace setbacks as learning opportunities. Reflect on the causes that contributed to the setback, identify lessons learned, and apply those lessons to future initiatives. This cyclical approach helps you learn and gain resilience.

7. *Take Action*: Instead of being paralyzed by setbacks, take aggressive measures towards fixing the challenges. Break the inertia by applying the tactics and solutions you've discovered. Action is crucial to achieving progress and moving forward.

8. *Celebrate Milestones and Progress*: Acknowledge and celebrate even the tiniest milestones and achievements along the road. Recognizing your progress promotes morale and provides the incentive to continue overcoming problems.

9. *Maintain Self-Care*: Take care of your physical and emotional well-being throughout the process. Engage in things that renew you and

create a sense of balance, such as exercise, meditation, or spending time with loved ones. Self-care builds your resilience and enhances your ability to overcome problems.

10. *Stay optimistic and Persevere*: Maintain an optimistic mindset and believe in your abilities to overcome problems. Cultivate tenacity and persistence, understanding that setbacks are fleeting and that with dedication, you may attain your goals.

By accepting these tactics, you can effectively negotiate setbacks and problems, transform them into chances for growth, and ultimately achieve success in various facets of life.

ADAPTING AND MAKING CHANGES FOR SUCCESS

Adapting and making changes is a transforming process that propels individuals towards achievement. It demands a proactive strategy to accept new chances, modify strategies, and learn from experiences. By thoroughly examining your current conditions, you can discover areas that demand improvement and design a complete plan for change.

Seeking support from mentors or experts provides vital direction and insights, helping you overcome obstacles efficiently. It's vital to retain a flexible mentality, which allows you to pivot when necessary and embrace fresh viewpoints. Taking persistent action, monitoring progress, and making appropriate modifications enable you to stay on course towards your goals.

Embracing a philosophy of lifelong learning fosters personal growth and allows you to continually adapt and prosper. By celebrating milestones and appreciating progress, you promote drive and reinforce positive improvements. Through this transforming process of adaptation and change, you unlock your potential and set the course for permanent success. Ultimately, by preparing yourself for long-term success and fulfillment.

CHAPTER 5

HARNESSING INNOVATION AND CREATIVITY

Harnessing your imaginative and creative force is incredibly advantageous for several reasons:
One significant advantage is problem-solving. By tapping into your imagination, you can approach challenges from multiple angles, think outside the box, and generate innovative solutions.

Embracing your creative and innovative qualities also boosts your adaptability. In a continuously changing world, being able to adapt and uncover new possibilities is vital. Creativity permits you to think creatively in unforeseen situations and respond with novel ideas.

Furthermore, increasing your creative and innovative power gives you a competitive advantage. It helps you stand out by introducing unique ideas and insights to your business, setting you apart from others.

On a personal level, fostering your creativity encourages growth and self-expression. It helps you explore your passions, test your limits, and find your unique talents and strengths. It can add a sense of fulfillment and purpose to your life.

Creativity and invention also thrive in collaborative contexts. By leveraging your creative power, you may contribute to team initiatives, inspire people with your ideas, and promote a culture of innovation. Collaborating with various people can lead to revolutionary outcomes.

Moreover, embracing your creative and imaginative abilities stimulates constant learning. It encourages you to seek new knowledge, examine emerging trends, and keep informed in your industry. This continual quest for knowledge fuels personal and professional growth.

Lastly, creativity and innovation have the ability to have a positive impact on society. By using your creative power, you can discover unique solutions to address social, environmental, and economic concerns. Your thoughts and contributions can generate substantial change.

In summary, embracing and fostering your innovative and creative capacity allows for successful problem-solving, boosts adaptability, provides a competitive edge, promotes personal growth, stimulates teamwork, supports continual learning, and enables positive impact. By tapping into your creative potential, you uncover prospects for growth and contribute to a more innovative future.

ENCOURAGING CREATIVE THINKING

Creative thinking is a strong catalyst for releasing our imaginative potential and driving innovation. When we build an environment that supports and nurtures creativity, we empower individuals to go beyond the ordinary, explore unknown territory, and come up with groundbreaking ideas. It starts with developing curiosity, encouraging individuals to ask questions, challenge assumptions, and explore different views. By embracing a philosophy of openness and exploration, we provide space for innovative ideas to develop.

Collaboration has a key function in stimulating innovative thinking. When varied perspectives and experiences come together, they contribute a plethora of ideas and insights that can spark new connections and inspire inventive solutions. By building a culture of collaboration, where employees feel comfortable sharing their opinions and participating in projects, we magnify the possibility for creative breakthroughs.

In this creative environment, it is vital to celebrate and embrace mistakes and failures as valuable learning experiences. By reducing the fear of judgment and supporting a development mentality, individuals are more likely to take chances, experiment, and iterate on their ideas. This iterative method enables ongoing improvement and refinement, leading to new outputs.

Furthermore, providing individuals with the flexibility to explore their passions and interests feeds their creative thinking. Allowing time for unstructured and self-directed exploration encourages individuals to dive into their particular talents and areas of interest, resulting in fresh insights and inventive ideas.

By promoting creative thinking, we develop a culture of innovation where individuals are encouraged to realize their full creative potential.

This not only drives personal and professional growth but also feeds advancement in numerous technologies Creative thinking contributes to the invention of new products, services, and technology that address societal concerns and improve our lives.

In conclusion, building an environment that supports creative thinking is vital for unleashing creativity and promoting positive change. By welcoming curiosity, enabling collaboration, honoring mistakes, and giving chances for self-expression, we encourage individuals to tap into their creative potential and produce groundbreaking ideas. By nurturing a culture of creativity and invention, we can design a future that is distinguished by continual development and revolutionary solutions.

TRY NEW IDEAS AND APPROACHES

Trying new ideas and techniques is a great strategy to stimulate innovation and drive personal and professional progress. By moving outside of our comfort zones and embracing the unfamiliar, we open ourselves up to new opportunities and fresh views.

When we attempt new ideas, we challenge the status quo and break away from conventional thinking. This allows us to explore novel ideas and unearth untapped potential. It motivates us to think creatively and discover innovative responses to issues. Even if these ideas don't always work, they provide essential learning experiences that contribute to our growth and development.

Similarly, attempting new techniques entails breaking away from established routines and processes. It entails experimenting with different tactics, techniques, and instruments to attain our aims. By embracing a philosophy of experimenting, we can unearth more efficient, productive, and inventive ways of doing things.

Trying new ideas and techniques also helps us adapt to change and remain nimble in a continually shifting world. It permits us to navigate through unclear situations and choose alternative paths when presented with problems. By being open to new possibilities, we can seize chances that may have otherwise been neglected.

Moreover, trying new ideas and approaches cultivates a culture of constant learning and progress. It pushes us to seek out new knowledge, learn new skills, and stay updated on evolving trends and innovations. This continual learning approach supports our personal and professional progress, develops our capacities, and positions us at the forefront of innovation.

Trying new ideas and techniques is crucial for stimulating creativity, generating growth, and adjusting to change. By embracing the unknown, trying alternative tactics, and keeping open to new ideas, we unlock our creative potential and unearth inventive solutions. Embracing an attitude of constant learning and progress moves us ahead on the path of personal and professional success.

USING TECHNOLOGY TO YOUR ADVANTAGE

In today's digital economy, utilizing the power of technology is important for developing a firm and establishing a competitive edge. Leveraging technology allows organizations to streamline processes, access a wider audience, and drive growth. One major part is leveraging digital marketing tactics such as **search engine optimization** (SEO), social media marketing, and online advertising to boost brand awareness and attract potential clients.

Additionally, deploying customer relationship management (CRM) systems and automation tools can expedite sales and customer support procedures, resulting in better efficiency and enhanced customer satisfaction. Embracing e-commerce platforms enables firms to increase their market reach and tap into worldwide marketplaces, giving simple online purchasing experiences for customers. Data analytics solutions provide significant insights into customer behaviour, preferences, and industry trends, helping organizations to make informed decisions and modify their strategy accordingly.

Cloud-based collaboration tools and project management software promote successful communication and collaboration among team members, regardless of their physical location. By embracing technology, businesses may achieve scalability, streamline operations, improve client experiences, and establish a competitive advantage in the digital market.

Embracing technology is no longer an option but a need for businesses to flourish and win in today's highly competitive industry.
Strategically deploying technology to your advantage demands careful preparation and

implementation. Here are simplified steps to consider:

1. *Set clear goals*: Define your business objectives and identify places where technology can assist you achieve them.

2. *Assess your present technology*: Evaluate your existing systems and procedures to discover any gaps or places for improvement.

3. *Research and prioritize:* Look for technology solutions that meet your goals and budget. Focus on the ones that can have the most impact and are easy to integrate.

4. *Create an implementation strategy*: Make a clear plan with actions, money, and deadline. Communicate it clearly to your team.

5. *Foster a technology-friendly culture*: Encourage your employees to embrace technology by showcasing its benefits, giving training, and boosting cooperation.

6. *Monitor and evaluate*: Keep an eye on how the technology is functioning for you. Use statistics to measure progress and make educated decisions.

7. *Stay adaptable and up-to-date*: Stay open to new technology and adjust as needed to stay competitive.

By following these basic steps, you can strategically leverage technology to improve your business processes, increase client experiences, and drive development.

CULTIVATING AN INNOVATIVE CULTURE

Cultivating an inventive culture in an organization is vital for promoting innovation and ongoing growth. Here are simplified techniques to help you build an inventive culture:

1. *Embrace a Growth Mindset*: Encourage staff to perceive problems as chances to learn and grow. Value inquiry, exploration, and resilience.

2. *Promote Collaboration and Diversity*: Create a collaborative environment where varied perspectives can come together. Encourage teamwork and open communication to exchange ideas.

3. *Encourage Risk-Taking and Experimentation*: Create a safe place where employees feel comfortable taking risks and trying new things. Emphasize learning from both accomplishments and setbacks.

4. *Provide Resources and Support*: Give staff the tools and training they need for creativity and innovation. Invest in technology and offer mentorship programs.

5. *Recognize and Reward Innovation*: Acknowledge and applaud innovative thinking. Implement recognition programs to motivate personnel.

6. ***Foster a Learning Culture***: Encourage ongoing learning and knowledge-sharing. Provide access to training and assist employees' professional development.

7. ***Lead by Example***: Show leadership commitment to innovation. Create a supportive environment where employees feel empowered to take chances and explore innovative solutions. You should endeavour to create an environment where creativity thrives, issues are solved in novel ways, and new ideas blossom.

CHAPTER 6

SCALING UP FOR SUCCESS

Scaling up for success as a newbie entrepreneur might be a difficult task, but it is surely doable with the appropriate approach and mindset. To begin, as I have previously stated in this book, it is critical to validate your business idea by conducting thorough market research and testing your product or service with a small group of clients; their comments will help you refine your offering before expanding further.

It is also critical to lay a solid foundation. Concentrate on improving essential components of your company, such as your value proposition, customer experience, and operational processes. Create a robust infrastructure, invest in necessary resources, and build a skilled team to support your expansion objectives.

Another important factor I've discussed is leveraging technology. Embrace tools and platforms that can automate operations, improve productivity, and increase your potential to scale. Accounting, project management, and customer relationship management software that is cloud-based can be especially valuable. It is also critical to create a scalable business plan. Evaluate your operations to discover potential bottlenecks or locations where growth may be hampered. As you grow, streamline procedures, manage resource allocation, and plan for rising demand.

Developing a growth strategy is critical for scaling up. Outline your expansion goals, methods, and tactics. Establish quantifiable goals, critical milestones, and a timetable for accomplishing them. Seek help and mentorship from seasoned entrepreneurs or mentors who have scaled their own businesses. To gain access to significant resources, join local entrepreneurial networks, attend industry events, and consider joining an incubator or accelerator program.

Securing appropriate money is frequently required for scaling up. Consider options such as angel investors, venture capital, crowdfunding, or small company loans for finance. Prepare a compelling business strategy and proposal that illustrates your venture's development potential.

Monitor important metrics related to your growth goals and make data-driven decisions based on the results. Finally, adjust to your experiences and learn from them. Accept feedback, improve your product or service, and remain dedicated to quality and client pleasure. As a first-time entrepreneur, you can boost your chances of success by maintaining a growth mentality and perseverance.

CREATING A SCALABLE BUSINESS MODEL

Creating a scalable business plan is critical for achieving long-term growth and successfully scaling up your company. A scalable company model allows you to raise revenue and profitability without increasing expenditures and resources proportionally. The following are critical steps in developing a scalable company model:

1. *Identify a Market Need*: Begin by finding a major and unmet market need. Look for problems, gaps, or inefficiencies that your product or service can solve. A scalable business model is built on a substantial market need.

2. *Define Your Value Proposition*: Clearly describe the distinct benefit that your product or service provides to customers. Identify the primary advantages, benefits, or solutions it offers above existing options. A powerful value proposition distinguishes your company and attracts customers.

3. *Target a certain Market Segment*: Rather than attempting to serve everyone, focus on a certain market segment or niche. By restricting your target group, you may more effectively personalize your service to match their individual demands. This strategy enables more targeted marketing efforts and increased customer interaction.

4. *Utilize Technology and Automation:* To streamline operations and boost efficiency, incorporate technology and automation into your business processes. This can include deploying digital tools, software platforms, or e-commerce

capabilities. Automation reduces expenses and allows for scalability.

5. ***Create a Repetitive and Standardized procedure***: Establish a standardized procedure for delivering your product or service. As you scale, this ensures consistency and quality. To preserve efficiency and effectiveness, document your procedures, train workers, and set protocols.

6. ***Consider Strategic Partnerships and Outsourcing***: To utilize knowledge and resources without making large investments, consider strategic partnerships or outsourcing specific services. Collaboration with complementary firms or the outsourcing of non-core operations can help to speed growth and scalability.

7. ***Create a Revenue Model***: Create a revenue model that allows for scalability. Consider subscription-based models, recurring revenue, licensing fees, or other kinds of monetization

that will provide a consistent and predictable income stream as your business grows.

8. *Scalability planning* is anticipating future development and planning your infrastructure and resources accordingly. Ascertain that your systems, processes, and technology are capable of handling additional demand without serious disruptions. Scalability should be integrated into your business model from the ground up.

9. *Continuous Improvement and Adaptation*: Evaluate your business model regularly, solicit input from customers and stakeholders, and be willing to make necessary changes. Look for methods to improve your offering, operational efficiency, and client experience regularly.

10. *Establish key performance indicators (KPIs)* to assess your progress and evaluate the success of your scalable company strategy. client acquisition costs, client lifetime value, revenue growth, and profitability are all variables to keep an eye on. Make informed decisions with data-driven insights.

Keep in mind that creating a scalable company model is an iterative process. It necessitates continuous examination, refinement, and change in response to market dynamics and client input. As you scale your business, stay agile, sensitive to market developments, and devoted to providing value to your customers.

OPERATIONS AND PROCESSES OPTIMIZATION

Optimizing operations and processes is a vital step toward increasing efficiency, lowering expenses, and laying the groundwork for scalable growth in your company. By optimizing your operations, you may increase efficiency, improve customer happiness, and lay a solid foundation for future growth.

Begin by finding areas for improvement in your current operations through a thorough assessment. Look for bottlenecks, inefficiencies, and areas where workflows can be streamlined and redundancies eliminated. Ensure uniformity and decrease errors by standardizing procedures. Use technology to automate jobs and optimize processes, such as project management software or CRM software.

Encourage good communication and collaboration within your organization to break down silos and promote teamwork. Invest in employee education to improve their skills and expertise. Monitor performance continuously, utilizing key metrics to find areas for improvement and make data-driven decisions.

Adopt a culture of continual improvement and think about outsourcing or partnerships to tap into specific expertise or free up resources. To stay ahead of the curve and enhance operational efficiency, keep up to current on industry trends and best practices. You can improve your company's overall performance and readiness for scalable growth by streamlining its operations and processes.

Optimizing operations and procedures is a complex approach that goes beyond simply increasing efficiency and lowering costs. It has the potential to supply your company with a variety of benefits and perspectives.

One of the most significant advantages is the opportunity to improve overall customer experience by streamlining procedures and assuring smooth interactions. From initial contact through product delivery, effective operations encourage loyalty and attract new consumers by creating a good and smooth customer journey. Furthermore, improved operations provide agility and adaptability, allowing your company to adjust to market changes swiftly, capitalize on new possibilities, and traverse problems more successfully.

Furthermore, effective processes promote scalability and expansion, guaranteeing that your company may expand without sacrificing quality or incurring exorbitant costs. You may strategically deploy resources, reinvest capital, and improve profitability by identifying areas for cost reduction and resource optimization.

This, in turn, helps your competitive edge by providing competitive prices, excellent customer satisfaction, and operational excellence. When customers sense superior efficiency and value, they are more inclined to choose your company over competitors.

Additionally, pursuing operational efficiency develops a culture of continual development inside your company. Employees are encouraged to offer suggestions, identify areas for improvement, and work together on process improvement efforts. This empowers your employees, improves engagement, and fosters an innovative attitude at all levels of the firm.

Finally, optimizing operations and procedures is a strategic imperative that has a broad impact on your firm. It promotes competitiveness, improves the customer experience, and fosters a culture of continual development. By embracing streamlining and harnessing technology, you prepare your company for long-term success in a volatile market.

HIRING AND CREATING A STRONG TEAM

A powerful team can propel creativity, productivity, and overall growth. To do so, you must first define your team's specific needs and determine the necessary talents, experience, and positions. To recruit top personnel, create an appealing employer brand that highlights your company's values, mission, and culture. Create an efficient recruitment process that includes properly screening candidates, conducting interviews, and analyzing their abilities and qualifications.

Cultural fit is also vital, so look for people who share your company's values and can contribute positively to the workplace. Prioritize diversity and inclusiveness as well to develop creativity and a diverse spectrum of perspectives. To recruit and retain top talent, offer competitive remuneration and benefits packages, as well as complete onboarding and training to assist their integration and development.

Encourage team members to collaborate and communicate, and set up mechanisms for regular feedback and performance reviews. Recognize outstanding performance to motivate and incentivize your workforce. Building a successful team is an ongoing effort, monitoring dynamics, solving difficulties, and making required modifications frequently to maintain ongoing success. Building a great team through successful hiring processes is a critical component of corporate success.

A strong and competent workforce may move a firm forward by encouraging innovation and accomplishing common goals. To construct such a team, it is critical to understand your organization's particular demands as well as the precise talents and attributes necessary in team members. Creating a strong employer brand is also important; it helps recruit top-tier personnel who share the company's values and objectives.

The recruitment process must be well-designed and efficient for you to thoroughly evaluate candidates and identify the greatest fit for each post. Individuals who share the company's values and can thrive within its work environment contribute to a peaceful and productive team dynamic. Prioritizing diversity and inclusion during the hiring process can bring new perspectives and ideas to the team.

Once the team has been assembled, it is critical to invest in their growth and development through training and onboarding. Offering competitive pay and benefits indicates your dedication to recognizing and appreciating your employees' accomplishments. Open communication and collaboration establish a healthy work environment in which team members may freely exchange ideas and work together to overcome obstacles.

Recognizing and applauding team members' accomplishments instills gratitude and inspires them to continue delivering excellent performance. Regularly monitoring team dynamics and providing constructive feedback aids in the resolution of issues and assures continual progress.

Building a great team is a continuous process that demands continuous effort and attention. It is critical to adapt and make required adjustments as the team grows and evolves to maintain an effective and cohesive entity. Finally, a strong team serves as the basis for a successful business by driving innovation, supporting growth, and paving the road to long-term success.

EXPANDING YOUR MARKET AND INCREASING SALES

Expanding your market and increasing sales are critical initiatives for companies seeking long-term success and profitability. You may improve revenue, strengthen market presence, and acquire a competitive edge by successfully contacting new customers and optimizing sales possibilities. Here is a more complete and comprehensive look at market expansion and sales strategies:

1. *Conduct Thorough Market Research*: Thorough market research is the cornerstone for successful market expansion. Investigate customer behaviour, preferences, and emerging trends in depth. Understand your target audience's wants and problem areas, and find untapped client niches. This study will inform your marketing and sales tactics.

2. *Create a Comprehensive Marketing Strategy*: Create a strategic marketing plan that combines traditional and digital marketing channels. To increase brand visibility, generate leads, and drive visitors to your business, use targeted advertising, content marketing, social media, influencer collaborations, and SEO tactics. Adapt your messaging and promotions to different client segments.

3. *Product and service differentiation*: Set yourself apart from the competition by stressing your products' or services' distinctive characteristics, benefits, or value propositions. Determine what sets you apart and effectively communicate these differentiators to your target audience. Highlight the benefits and value that customers will receive by picking your offerings above others on the market.

4. *Increase Distribution Channels*: Look for ways to increase your distribution channels and reach new clients. Consider forming alliances with retailers, distributors, or online marketplaces to gain access to new market segments. To increase your geographical reach, consider the possibility of international marketplaces or e-commerce platforms. Adapt your distribution strategy to fit the demands and preferences of various consumer categories.

5. *Create Strategic alliances:* Look for strategic alliances with firms or influencers whose products or services complement yours. Collaborate with businesses or individuals who have a similar target audience but sell non-competitive items. These collaborations can expose your business to new customer segments, raise brand awareness, and generate mutual referrals.

6. *Implement Customer Relationship Management (CRM):* Invest in a strong CRM system to successfully manage customer interactions and boost sales. A CRM system assists you in tracking and analyzing client data, purchasing trends, and preferences. Use this data to tailor communication, anticipate consumer

needs, and provide amazing customer experiences that lead to repeat sales and loyalty.

7. *Establish Customer Loyalty Programs*: Establish customer loyalty programs to reward and incentivize repeat purchases. To encourage continued participation and brand loyalty, provide unique discounts, prizes, or VIP privileges. Implement referral programs to capitalize on the power of word-of-mouth marketing and grow your customer base through recommendations from happy consumers.

8. *Improve the Sales Process:* To enhance conversion rates, constantly improve your sales process. Train and empower your sales team to explain the value of your products or services effectively. Provide regular sales training, provide the necessary tools and resources, and encourage a customer-centric attitude. Streamline the sales process to provide clients with a smooth and efficient experience.

9. ***Deliver Exceptional Customer Service***: Make exceptional customer service a priority to develop good experiences and strong customer relationships. Respond quickly to enquiries and concerns, and go above and above to surpass client expectations. Invest in customer service training and equip your employees to provide tailored assistance. Customers that are pleased with a product or service become brand champions, resulting in repeat purchases and good referrals.

10. ***Analyze and Optimize***: Analyze sales data, customer input, and market trends regularly to find opportunities for improvement. Use analytics tools to learn about customer behaviour and preferences. Adapt your plans based on the data collected, whether it's modifying price, refining target audience segments, launching new marketing campaigns, or experimenting with new sales approaches.

Finally, by following these tactics, you can broaden your market reach, attract new clients, and increase revenue. Monitor industry developments regularly, keep flexible, and change your approach to match changing customer wants. With a customer-centric approach, an extensive marketing strategy, and dedication.

CONCLUSION

It can be tempting to regard inefficiency as a weakness and avoid making mistakes while working towards your business mission. However, inefficiency is frequently an indication of inexperience and a lack of willingness to put in the necessary effort to make things function. This thinking can both paralyze and impede you from progressing.

To harness your beginner's attitude, you must first build a foundation of knowledge that will help you enhance your business and raise your chances of success. The more you understand about your sector, the more you will be able to play to your strengths as an entrepreneur. From there, you can make informed decisions about what works, what doesn't, and what you need to do to make your business a success.

The key to a successful career as a business visionary is to lay a solid educational foundation that will allow you to grow and improve over time. Even when you think you've learned everything there is to know, there are always new lessons to learn and new opportunities to grab.

Accepting the beginner's mindset is a critical step towards business success. It is about being open and eager to learn, regardless of your level of experience. It's all about being interested, asking questions, and being open to new experiences. Instead of assuming you already know everything, approach situations with an open mind and a willingness to learn.

When you embrace the beginner's mindset, you recognize that there is always something new to learn and that making mistakes is natural. You're open to feedback and seek advice from those who can help you grow. You are not afraid to step outside of your comfort zone and think differently. It facilitates the release of your creativity, adaptability, and potential. You are not limited by what you already know or what others expect of you. It is a continuous attitude of growth and learning that allows you to uncover new opportunities and achieve greater achievement in life.

Building a solid support network is critical to the success of any organisation. It is a calculated decision that can accelerate your progress, provide useful insights, and open doors to new prospects. A strong support network comprises mentors, industry peers, competent professionals, and potential investors who all contribute to the growth of your business.

Mentors provide advice based on their experience, assisting you in navigating problems and making educated decisions. Peers in the industry foster a sense of camaraderie, enabling knowledge sharing and collaboration. Skilled employees contribute experience in important areas, ensuring that your company is ready to tackle complicated projects. And investors can give you the capital you need to fund your expansion objectives.

Building a support network necessitates active participation, networking, and a genuine desire to contribute to the success of others. Entrepreneurs may tap into a wide pool of resources, guidance, and possibilities by building genuine relationships and reciprocal support. A solid support network functions as a catalyst in this interconnected business world, allowing organizations to develop and succeed in an ever-changing market.

It is difficult to sustain resilience in today's fast-paced workplace. It's critical to take care of yourself and find strategies to keep centred and focused. Maintain a journal or a blog to reflect on your experiences and analyse them in light of the lessons you've learned. This will help you stay motivated and eventually conquer the obstacles that life throws at you.

When confronted with difficulties, it is critical to have a growth mindset. Through the process of continuous learning and progress, this perspective assists you in increasing your resilience and positive energy. It's also critical to have a strong support system by surrounding yourself with individuals who inspire you and provide constructive feedback.

Businesses must transition from a traditional sales-driven methodology to a customer-centric one. A truly scalable organization must be able to grow while upholding its basic principles and quality standards. This is not a simple task. It takes a strong corporate leader who is willing to change course along the way. To help their firm succeed, it takes a leader that knows business fundamentals and is willing to engage in learning new skills and resources.

Before you begin expanding your business, take a step back and evaluate what has worked so far. Consider whether you have the necessary abilities, resources, income, and motivation to achieve your objectives. If you don't believe you do, it's time to rethink your objectives and make changes as needed. Scaling up your business means making the right investments.

It is possible to build your business regardless of how much or how little funding you have. While some technology and solutions do not require huge expenditures and hence may be more appropriate for a small business owner, other tools and toolkits can significantly improve your company's performance and reduce operational costs.

A well-designed scalable company model enables you to increase revenue and profitability without proportionally increasing expenditures and resources.

Congratulations, and I wish you luck on your new journey to success.

Thank you for reading this book, if you enjoy this book, kindly leave a review for it on Amazon to encourage the Author to write more of its kind.